BUDDHA IN ...

FINDING PEACE IN CHAOS

Pradeep Soundararajan

Illustrations by Padmashree Jayachandran

INDIA • SINGAPORE • MALAYSIA

Notion Press

Old No. 38, New No. 6
McNichols Road, Chetpet
Chennai - 600 031

First Published by Notion Press 2020
Copyright © Pradeep Soundararajan 2020
All Rights Reserved.

ISBN 978-1-64760-851-4

Dedicated to all the people
who test and care about testing.

The list of people I thank and credit
are at the end of this book

There are smarter people than me.

No code snippets in this book.

You can disagree with me and still be friends.

CONTENTS

Contents

WHY?

Buddha statues and photos are everywhere. From homes, hotels, spas, resorts, restaurants, office spaces to art galleries. Buddha has become a symbol of inner peace.

⊚ Why Are People Obsessed About Keeping a Buddha Everywhere?

Buddha reminds people to be calm, nice, and at peace.

⊚ Why Do People Need Reminders to Be Calm, Nice and at Peace?

Media and social media thrive on conditioning human behavior. Conditioning can invoke insecurity, fear and greed, leading to certain desires and certain buying patterns. Fear and insecurity can be systematically fed to create a certain desired behavior. Every time an organization achieves a desired behavior there are side effects to it. The side effects are the undesired behaviors.

Facebook is a great example. I too, was obsessed with it. The noise grew and grew until one day it became so high that I could no longer dismiss it. Most of us, including me, have stopped/paused Facebook or some other social media at least once before getting back into it. We decided to do so when the noise levels became too high. Even at that moment - we did not ask, "What did we do to create the noise?"

Quitting Facebook is easy but quitting the behavior of creating and amplifying noise continues to happen in our mind. It is hard to uninstall apps that our mind has built due to conditioning.

People today need reminders to be calm and nice to each other. Social media forums, be it about profession or politics, have people abusing each other in the name of "What is right?". Friends are becoming enemies or in the worst case - people are not discovering the human side of each other. There is enough hatred being spread and we are becoming lonelier. This is against being human.

◉ Why Buddha in Testing?

Testing is in a highly chaotic state, much more than how it was when I started my career 16 years ago. Functional Testers no longer believe they have a future and yet the world does need them. Large scale UI automation without fixing the layers of testability results in flakiness and results in high maintenance cost to the extent that the cost exceeds the value. Yet, people are obsessed with it.

A large percentage of developers who should be doing unit testing, either don't do it or don't want to.

Business and management are blind, thinking if something is automated, it has to be right. Hands-on testers are branded as QA - making the whole organization think there is a dedicated team to assure quality and it is not the responsibility of the people building it. There are QA teams even in organizations that say "Quality is everyone's responsibility". What does QA mean then?

Even learning in testing is driven by fear. A lot of people learn things to find their next best job rather than to solve problems at their current workplace. People want to learn tools that help them get jobs and not tools that solve the problem.

Some people are saying, thinking and also living by the idea that testing as a role will go away.

Over the last few years, I have been living in absolute inner peace about testing. I am no longer searching for answers. The answers I found have brought me peace. I also recognize that not everything I know will be good enough. I don't conclude. I don't judge. I don't fear that I will be judged. I don't fear losing. I am learning. I have been more peaceful in failure than with my success. Not that I don't aspire.

I do talk to a lot of people. I am active online. I am in the middle of all the chaos happening in testing. I run a business in testing. I speak at conferences and organizations. I am a beneficiary and equally a victim of this chaos.

A decade ago, I used to be macho just like many others. I would put people down when they didn't agree with me. That is animal behavior. I was revered for it. With grace and kindness showered on me, I was able to realize that we are celebrating wild animal behavior instead of celebrating being human.

Having transformed from being a wild animal in Testing to being human, I think it is my duty to pay it forward.

⑥ How Did I Transform?

I was logically right with many things I did (just like everyone else). And anytime I failed, I wondered why the failure happened despite being logically right. This caused a lot of unrest in my mind. The unrest led to a search outside of logic and I discovered that there is a realm beyond logic that can bring peace. I went in search of what defies logic and yet answers the many questions I had.

⑥ What Is That Something Else?

Spirituality. That is what connects all of us together. In non-religious spirituality, there exist answers, to questions that have bothered us. In spirituality exists what we need to be calm and peaceful. In spirituality exists ways for us to discover the humaneness in us. In spirituality exists

Buddhism, Adiyogi, Sadhguru Jaggi Vasudev, Sri Sri Ravishankar, Jiddu Krishnamurthy, Swami Sukhabodanda and Ryan Holiday have been complementary to each other in helping me bring peace to myself.

Buddha in Testing is an outcome of what makes me peaceful in Testing.

Buddha in Testing is an outcome of my care for people who care about testing and should be peaceful, but are not.

⑥ Why a Book and not a Series of Blogs?

There are enough good books, blogs and people today that can bring clarity on testing approaches, methodologies, test techniques etc., but none that focuses on how people who test can achieve peace amidst the chaos.

I wanted to remind people who test and care about it to be calm and peaceful - without which no amount of results is going to bring peace.

I wanted to tell them there are people out there who are out of chaos and living in inner peace - within the testing space. Not everyone might write a book and I wish they did.

I wanted to say - find your own Buddha. Find your own path to inner peace in this chaotic, testing world. Anything I write, I ask myself, will I enjoy reading it - had someone else written this? Similarly, I felt I would enjoy reading this as a book rather than a series of blog posts. Hence this book. Sorry to Mother Earth for all the paper (trees) that will be used to print this. I just hope it is worth those trees. As a gratitude to those trees, I would get 1 tree sapling planted for every 50 books printed.

THE CONSTRUCT OF THIS BOOK

⑥ Writing Experience

Over the last few years, my posts on LinkedIn and Quora have been fairly well read, liked, shared and argued over.

I have been able to test a variety of content related to testing through these posts and have had the pleasure of looking into the emotions expressed by people, the arguments, the debates, the sentiments, the disagreements and the support and love people have offered.

For whatever reason, in the last year, my total post views must have crossed 10 million. Reactions such as likes, comments, shares to the posts I put out might be 50K. I am not counting them but speculating based on what I have seen in the analytics.

Surprisingly, the maximum readership of my content is software developers. I have been absolutely surprised by it. I thought only Testers would be interested in my posts. Even now I am surprised as I write it.

A good number of people have messaged me that my posts were very helpful to them and they made a positive impact on software quality in their organization. A small number of people also wrote to me that they are upset with my content.

Sometimes people have made fun of me, publicly, on the posts I put out. Long ago when I had no visible gray hair, I would fight with them online. Today, with the graying that is visible, I handle disagreement with peace. I try to be helpful even with people who make fun of me.

I have gained a few friends that way. Someone who started with a comment that had a slight personal attack on me - ended up writing to me that I won over their heart because instead of focusing on the attack - I focused on the content and tried helping them. I too get swayed by emotions. That happens 1% of all the noise I immerse myself in. It used to be 99%.

This book certainly has the learning from the experience of having written to an audience that consists of software developers, testers and managers. I didn't write this book any differently from the way I have written my posts.

As a matter of fact, I am getting this book copy edited in a way that preserves my original writing style but fix some typos and grammatical mistakes I end up committing. I can hide behind calling English not as my first language but that doesn't mean the standard of writing has to be low. People whose first language is English can argue that some of my writing could have a more refined grammar if I had chosen a deeper form of copy editing. I just think I would like to write the way I have been writing since it is able to establish a connection with the audience.

Also, I am hoping this helps more people write books because they might be thinking that their English needs to be perfect before they can publish one.

I wish - they come to peace that their English is never going to be perfect.

I just hope my English is good enough.

⑥ Reading Experience

I know there are people like my wife who can read a Harry Potter and the Goblet of Fire 636-page book in 3 days. I would take 30. My reading style is - I have to read a few pages, go into my own dreamland, imagine all the beautiful things and mix them into my experience, construct stories, live in it for some time, get back to reality and repeat this cycle for every few pages.

I take book reading vacations. Over the last four years, at the end of every year, I go out on vacation and carry books to read before the year ends. December 29th, 30th and 31st usually go in reading books, sipping whiskey and spending the evenings with my family. It is a great way to clear my backlog for the year and with a hope to step into the New Year, smarter and with peace.

As a slow reader, I once had to extend my bookation (vacation) by a day because I couldn't complete reading the book I wanted to.

I would like this book to be a light read for anyone. If you are like my wife - you can finish reading this book in 3 hours. If you are like me, you could take 2 days. I want to pass your 1 day test before I can qualify to write something that can consume more of your time.

Equally, I don't think people have a large enough attention span these days.

Many bugs find us. We find very few.

Breathing is oblivious. So is chaos.

CHAPTER

FUNDAMENTALS OF TESTING

TESTING

- Someone has a business idea to solve a pain point across customers.
- That someone wants to build a product that solves the identified pain.
- That someone builds a product by hiring Product and Engineering Teams.
- That someone wants an internal feedback system about the Product.
- That someone has many questions in mind.
- That someone wants to know, "Are we ready to invest in marketing spend?"
- That someone wants to know if customers have obstacles in using the product.
- That someone wants to know if customers' pain is really solved through the product.
- That someone hopes everyone in the company evolves based on the feedback.
- The feedback loop to evolve is called Testing.

⊚ Chaos

Different people have different understanding and hence different definitions of Testing.

As time passes by on this Earth, people will keep coming up with new and more appealing definitions about testing than what exists today.

Some testers think testing is conformance, some think it is assuring quality, some think testing is improving the quality and some think it is finding information that influences stakeholders.

When these people talk to each other, they disagree with each other and produce materials that seem to conflict others ideas. Be it online or offline. No matter what definition you come up with there will be people who always subscribe to it.

The perfectly imperfect idea of "bug free product" has enough followers in this world even today.

⌇Inner Peace

- Testing is a feedback loop.
- Feedback = The product doesn't work as per requirements + The product requirements could be wrong + The Product violates user agreements + The Product first time user experience isn't great + The Product is inconsistent to claims + that + that + that…
- Everyone is right but in a narrow-shallow way. Some people seem broader than others.
- Don't argue with people about definitions.
- Speak through your work.
- Speak about your work.

AUTOMATION IN TESTING

- Someone wants to test a product.
- That someone wants to do a lot of tests.
- That someone wants to do a variety of tests.
- That someone wants to focus on more important things.
- That someone wants to bring in tools to improve test coverage.
- That someone wants to bring in technology that aids testing.
- The technology that aids in delivering this value is automation.

◎ Chaos

- Instead of seeing automation as a service to testing, the majority of the world started celebrating it as a replacement to testing.
- People who couldn't sell testing value found an opportunity to start promoting automation as a better approach than testing.
- Sadly, testers also caught up to it. They saw new job opportunities being created - more secure jobs and more tech kind of work, so it appealed to them. They all quit testing to get into automation.
- Today - most testers presenting about automation start by saying, "Manual Testing is slow". Reminding you of James and Michael in

37

Rapid Software Testing, would ask, "Slow compared to what? Manual Programming is slow too. Why not automate that?!"

〜 Inner Peace

Non-tech/Management

- These people think testing is an unnecessary opex.
- The manufacturing industry precedes the Software Industry.
- Automation is a well-known word used as a replacement for humans in Manufacturing.
- The word automation appeals to people.
- They don't know they are buying more human workforce in the name of automation.
- They don't know that the cost of maintenance of this automation can be huge.
- They just want to see the tests done by humans - no longer done by humans.
- They are duped into paying more to run similar tests at thrice the cost.

Geeks/CTO/VP Engineering

- For them everything is a tech problem.
- They love bringing technology to everything that they do.
- They love hiring developers.

- Automation is more tech than what Testing appears to be.
- Automation appeals to them.
- Automation gives them the notion of speed and it does offer speed to their work, done right.
- They love coding. Automation is coding.
- Testing isn't (well, sometimes).

Testers

- Most young folks lack the big picture of testing.
- Some wanted to be programmers but couldn't.
- They think automation gives them safety in a world where people think testing is a cost.
- This gives them hope for the future.
- Most of them don't have the background for automation.
- They create flaky frameworks and automation.
- They spend more time maintaining what they have built.

A.I. Folks

- Maintenance heavy automation is A.I.'s paradise.
- Today people are realizing the cost of maintenance of automation is high.
- Selling A.I. as a solution to reduce the cost of that maintenance works great.
- Developer's time spent debugging an automation failure hurts.
- A.I. fits in perfectly.

- Heal the problem we created.
- Again a programmer's paradise.
- The QA (as they want to call testers) aren't direct beneficiary of A.I. yet. Similar to how automation never came to help them but should have.
- Those who really understand automation and testing together hope that their voices are heard.

TEST COVERAGE

- Someone wants to make a release.
- They have a criterion for a release.
- They want to know if the software is release ready.
- They expect a test team to help them assess release readiness.
- Release readiness can be determined by asking questions such as:
  - What to test?
  - When to test that?
  - Why test that?
  - How much to test that?
  - How often should it be tested?
- Collective answers and actions based on:
  - What
  - Why
  - When
  - And How
  - Forms Test coverage

⑥ Chaos

Managers

- Most managers in the world think:
- Test coverage = Test case coverage.
- That is shallow thinking because...
- The test cases may be less, more, irrelevant, obsolete or different from the context required.

- Managers are under pressure to push a release out.
- Testers are expected to highlight the risks of poor test coverage.
- They don't. Instead they give a sign off under pressure.

Testers

- Testers are excited about bugs.
- They think finding bugs is the most important thing in testing.
- They don't understand that without good enough coverage finding too many bugs in one area could be useless.

∿ Inner Peace

- "Cover" means "Enclosing a certain area".
- Software, no matter how small - is always complex to test.
- Complete testing is impossible for any software
- We can't cover everything.
- Testing is sampling.
- Good testing = Right sampling.
- Right or wrong is determined by the context.
- Test Techniques, Heuristics and Oracles = Ways of sampling.
- Modeling = Ways of separating dimensions.
- Browser is a dimension, user is a dimension, first time user is another dimension.

- Tests = Experiments.
- Test Coverage =
  - Skills leading to
  - Understanding Context, leading to
  - Modeling, leading to
  - Techniques, leading to
  - Setup, leading to
  - Tests, leading to
  - Observations, leading to
  - Interpretation of Results, leading to
  - Influencing people
- Personally, I keep showing the value of this kind of thinking about test coverage to people and some of them end up working with me.

TESTABILITY

- Someone has written a piece of code.
- They want feedback on how the code works in different contexts.
- Those who test design experiments.
- Some experiments can't reach a certain portion of code.
- Some experiments can't be performed due to a limitation.
- Some experiment depth is compromised by the design.
- We need a mechanism to remove the limitation on testing.
- That mechanism is testability.
- To test it, we need to be able to control it.
- Control the environment.
- Control Input/Output.
- Control the dependencies.
- This controllability is testability.

⊚ Chaos

- Most testers don't know about testability.
- Some who knows don't know to ask for it.
- Some of those who ask aren't asking in an influential way.
- Testability becomes an overhead in many org cultures.

- Testability isn't usually a part of the story or the requirement.
- Testability has been impacting test coverage.
- When people find a bug in production,
- People rarely ask the question, "Did we make this testable?"
- Testability is partially addressed during automation.
- Automation engineers are struggling to get the element ids they need.
- Most automation ends up as compromised patch work.

∿ Inner Peace

- As a tester - I want to run a lot of different kinds of experiments.
- Some experiments are straight forward.
- Pass the input - assess the output.
- Some experiments are not straight forward.
- Pass the input - interrupt the processing - assess the output.
- If the interruption mechanism doesn't exist - I need help.
- If I know how to code - I do it on my own.
- If I don't know, I need to know how to ask for help.
- I need to master the art of asking and getting help.

- I have got enough help from developers and automation engineers.
- I got a lot of instrumentation done before I test software.
- What I ask them to build and the way I influence them to build, has helped them build respect for me as a tester.
- Over the years, this has helped me become a Product Owner of Testing Tools.
- Today, I am looking to enable testability for other testers through tools like Bugasura.
- I am satisfied with my progression from a Tester to PO of Testing Tools.

FUNCTIONAL TESTING

- A product solves a series of problems under the same umbrella.
- A feature is a piece within the umbrella of the product.
- A feature solves a specific problem.
- The feature is made up of multiple individual components.
- These individual components are functions.
- They take input values and produce output.
- That output is either consumed by a user or another component.
- Eventually a user consumes the final output.
- People building these functions want answers to the following questions.
- Does the function solve the problem for the user?
- Does the function break when a new function is placed in tandem?
- Does the function break as new lines of code are added to it?
- Does the function break because a depending function breaks?

◎ Chaos

Some think Functional Testers,

- Need to be a domain expert.
- Need tech + domain skills.
- It should be automated.

- Has no learning in it over a period of time.
- Most see Functional Testing as an Input/Output comparison.
- Most see Functional Testing as a Checking Job.
- Industries such as Banking value domain knowledge more than Testing skills.
- They have quasi BA Testing done by Testers.
- They don't understand the value of pair-testing.
- Testers fail to enjoy Functional Testing.
- They think they aren't learning much.
- They think their lives have become monotonous.
- They think Performance Testing and Security Testing are sexier.

⌇Inner Peace

- Most people in testing make their living by doing Functional Testing.
- I spend a lot of time understanding the purpose.
- It makes sense to pick up and test a function or a feature only after understanding the purpose.
- I go back to the understanding that the function is f(x) = y.
- I don't look at Functional Testing just as an Input Output Analysis.
- I test:
    - ○ functions under various conditions.
    - ○ performance of a function in those conditions.

- o user reaction to a function's performance.
- o usefulness of an output to the user.
- o if the objective of building it was met.
- I have personally made functional testing a very exciting thing.
- There is certainly some checking involved over a period of time.
- Some part of the checking can be done by machines.
- Some part of the checking relating to human factors can only be done by humans.
- I get a fresh pair of eyes to do the checks every now and then.
- Domain knowledge helps but it isn't a blocker to start.
- Pairing up with BA, SME and Testing is very helpful.
- Having the necessary tech skills helps us go deeper.
- Pairing up with a developer helps too.
- Pairing improves learning.
- Companies who worry about productivity to the hour will have plenty of regression issues.
- Unless their culture changes - their fate isn't changing much.

REGRESSION TESTING

- Someone has built a software and released it to their users.
- They have got some feedback from users to fix things.
- Designers and developers fix it to the best of their capabilities.
- The software is so complex - they need answers to two questions.
- Have we really fixed it?
- Have we broken something by trying to fix these?
- Finding answers to these questions is Regression Testing.

⊚ Chaos

- The way industry practices Regression Testing = Run all test cases.
- The way testers see Regression Testing = "Oh, No, Not again."
- The coverage achieved in Regression Testing is limited.
- Most people want full regression automation.
- Most people think when they have automation - they are done with regression.
- The time given to testing teams to do regression testing is crunched.
- Due to the time crunch most testers perform poor coverage.

- Most testers stretch their timings to cover as much.
- Yet, it falls insufficient sometimes because some things need time.
- Once a bug is reopened due to a code change - it is highly likely it will be reopened again.
- If a bug is reopened too many times - the tester gets tired of it.
- Bugs rejoice.
- Most people retain their jobs because regression exists.

～Inner Peace

- I do regression testing the non-boring way.
- I start with a risk assessment.
- Risk of a bug.
- Risk of a bug fix.
- Risk of a bug fix on other components.
- When working in a team,
- I let the testers who want to run a lot of checks do the checking.
- I let the automation suite run.
- I spend time finding out what got fixed, who reported it, why they reported it.
- I spend time with the developers to understand how they fixed it.
- I spend time reading code.
- I am not a coding guru but the code is English, thankfully.

- If I don't have access to the code - I have some previous build behavior notes.
- I do a bit of consistency checks myself.
- I then delve into impact mapping.
- I test for impact fixes on the rest of the system.
- If bug fixes are in components heavily used - I need more time.
- If bug fixes are in components that are less used - I can live with medium depth testing.
- I think people are heavily confused about regression testing.
- That isn't going to change soon.
- They are yielding to pressure.
- It is hard for humans to not yield to pressure.
- Building quality into software means not yielding to pressure at times.
- I build impact and risk dashboards for regression testing.
- I have automated go-no-go decisions.

PERFORMANCE TESTING

- Someone wants to build a product to solve a problem.
- There are two types of consumers/users for software: Humans and other software.
- Most humans are impatient.
- These humans expect software to work like humans.
- They want software to talk back at the speed a human would reply.
- They lose their interest in software if it is slow.
- They move to alternate software if the alternate converses faster.
- That someone who is building software wants answers to.
- Is my software slow?
- Why is it slow?
- What is slowing it down?
- Have my fixes improved the speed?
- The experiment to find answers to these questions is Performance Testing.

◎ Chaos

- A lot of people think Performance Testing is a phase.
- A lot of people think they will test for Performance after Functional stability.

- A lot of people think they can fix performance issues after Functional stability.
- A lot of people don't think Performance has a direct impact on UX.
- Testers think learning Performance Testing is learning Jmeter.
- Testers think Performance Testing is a full time job.
- Testers think adding tools like Jmeter will brighten their careers.
- Performance testing is not done end to end.
- People do server side and client side as two different activities.
- People sometimes compensate for software performance issues by increasing hardware.
- Most people think of it as a one-time activity.

~~Inner Peace

- Performance is a feature of Functionality.
- Performance is also a part of User Experience.
- There is real performance and perceived performance.
- There is never a single place where things are slow.
- Performance issues are due to a cascading effect.
- Performance testing is to be done in a highly systematic way.
- It starts by reviewing the architecture.
- Next comes the testability assessment.

- Performance testing isn't a phase.
- Benchmarking against competition is the last step - not the first.
- Benchmarking with previous builds is necessary and highly valuable.
- Code change to performance impact is a continuous testing activity.
- My compass keeps asking me, have I found answers to the following questions.
- Is the software slow?
- Why is it slow?
- What is slowing it down?
- Have the fixes improved the speed?
- Who am I supposed to talk to?
- Who needs to act on the information I provide?
- What information do they need?
- What would be the impact to the user?
- I build dashboards to understand what users were and are perceiving.
- Making an impact on users is more important than glorifying my CV with Jmeter.
- My inner peace comes from seeing the positive impact on customers and users.

UNIT TESTING

- Someone is writing a piece of code for a product.
- That someone wants to know if the code does what they thought it would.
- That someone wants to know if the code does anything else.
- That someone wants to know if it fails.
- That someone writes a test (usually another piece of code with test data).
- That someone builds the product code around the test code they have written.
- That someone uses the test as a reference when refactoring.

⊚ Chaos

- Many programmers think unit testing slows them down.
- Some programmers think they are pretty good they don't need unit tests.
- Many organizations try to bring the practice of unit testing by Devs at some point and fail.
- Testers find plenty of bugs that weren't supposed to be found by them.
- Testers find what is supposed to be found by unit testing.
- Most testers don't know how to push back.

- Lack of unit testing creates the need for more testers on many projects.
- Lack of unit testing creates testing jobs that makes testing look like a checking job.

⌒ Inner Peace

- Unit Testing, Integration Tests and Dev Testing are important to build quality.
- Testers are downstream and can't catch tons of bugs that slip unit testing.
- The potential of testers is yet to be tapped in a great way.
- No useful testing skills can be built in a place where no unit testing exists.
- People who talk about "everyone owns quality" should begin with unit testing.
- Having worked in such environments, today I advocate the debt we are paying with the lack of unit testing and find myself replacements or build a team of checkers to do my job.
- As a tester, in every bad engineering culture I have been exposed to, I have found there is always that one awesome person who is passionate and skilled but stuck there for some reason. I always partner with them for the good crimes we do together to help build quality and our own secret ways of doing things that people say to not but we know is important for the user.

- I should care about quality only as much as the people in the project care for. No more. More will harm my health. I should be ready to walk off any day without emotions. Working with people who care, is not work.

Long live unit testing!

The one person you keep
crossing often in your life is you.

CHAPTER

STATEMENTS

"YOU ARE OUR LAST LINE OF DEFENSE"

Certain organizational cultures tend to think of Testers as their last line of defense. What are these people defending? Defending bugs from going into production. Why do they want to defend? Bugs are plenty in their software and they know it. Instead of fixing their culture and themselves, they seem to find it easy to tell the testers to own up more than what they should and what they can. Fixing others is always easier than fixing ourselves (at least we think so).

⑥ Chaos

Organizations that tell testers they are the last line of defense mean - "You are our only hope because we can't fix this ourselves." That is a small part of the chaos. The chaos I am concerned about is Testers accepting it and finding pride in being the last line of defense.

I understand at some point most of us dreamt about being a uniformed soldier or admired one but even the uniformed soldiers on the border have to rely on intelligence agencies. If there is a failure of intelligence, the soldier on the border dies. It is teamwork and team ownership.

Testers accepting to be the last line of defense absolutely wreck their life. There is a very high pressure on them for every release. They think they are doing a lot of hard work and hence think they deserve to get more money. Testers in such context - rarely get satisfaction from their work. People keep telling them that it isn't good enough.

～ Inner Peace

If I were to find bugs, I would love to find the source of the bug. Most often the source of bugs exists in culture, recruitment, budgets, and the way people are communicating and behaving with each other. Many of my consulting reports have org problems listed in the test report.

I recognize that till the org and culture bugs are fixed - the software bugs will keep coming and my team and I can get tired of catching the same set of bugs over and over again. The bugs start to become oblivious - the testing starts to get boring.

Being the last line of defense is not something I take pride in. I have written emails to senior management as to how their lack of communication with their peers and their engineering culture is hurting the software quality.

My role moves from being a hands-on tester to being a quality advocate. So what? I am not in the job of saving my job. I am in the job of solving problems for software quality. If I want to solve problems, I would do what the organization requires but don't have.

In some contexts, the accumulated debt is so huge that the damage is irreversible.

I was testing a legacy system and every time someone fixed a bug, three new bugs were being introduced. No one knew the architecture. The best testing I ever did in this case was to tell the management - they don't need testing to find bugs in software unless they are thinking of re-building the whole application. They could use the test team in different ways to learn behavior than find bugs.

We started to contribute to the new cloud based system rather than testing the legacy software, while learning how the legacy system solved our customers problems. Life became peaceful. Otherwise, continuing to test a system like that leads us to a never ending loop would have kept our jobs going to the point the company shuts down.

WHY DID YOU MISS THIS BUG?

Classic. Age old. Still fresh. Still relevant. Some parts of the world are advancing and some parts of the world are still living in the Stone Age. How to answer questions posed by people from the Stone Age?

This follows the notion that testers are gatekeeping and during one of the gatekeeping sessions, they slept off and a bug danced over the gatekeeper and passed by without being noticed. So the question of, "You had one job and you couldn't do that?" comes up.

Such organizations produce a ton of bugs due to their bad practices and culture. You can catch bugs if they are few in number but if there are hundreds of bugs trying to cross over at the same time and you have two hands and an automation that checks only one bug at a time, how many bugs can you catch? So, it is likely you will miss more than what you catch.

◎ Chaos

A couple of things happen when such questions are asked. Some testers panic. Some testers feel obliged to accept their mistake. Some stakeholders think, "Why are we even paying for these gatekeepers who can't do a basic job?" And people get all worried, cancel their leaves and work harder.

The testers then get advice from everyone in the project on how to test. They start feeling bad about not having done a good job and try to do better the next time. This cycle never ends. Again, the Stone Age questions arise. Rinse repeat till you die or quit testing.

⌇Inner Peace

A bad tester might find 50 bugs.
A good tester might find 10 bugs.
A great tester might find 3 bugs.
An awesome tester might find just 1 bug.

It is not the number of bugs we find. It is the value and influence of the bugs we find. So in that sense, if there is a mother bug that is giving raise to hundreds of bugs, instead of being at the gate I would be deep inside the barn finding the nest.

This is what has kept me very peaceful and yes, I would miss bugs.

When I miss bugs, if someone asks me "Why did you miss that bug?", I would tell them "Have you done the RCA? There are many factors as to why a bug would occur in production. Would you like to join me in doing the RCA?". No matter how many times they ask me the question, I keep going to the question "Has the RCA been done?"

Usually people who ask these questions don't like to be challenged. They may react violently or they may react emotionally. They may try threatening or they may simply ignore.

They are the nest I have been looking for.

I hate being in a position where I have to report people as a nest. Sometimes I have done it when I have been in such a situation. Of course, I have had to absorb a loss. Getting used to such people is a bigger loss to my long term than a short term loss.

If the RCA reveals that I could have done better, I would take it in my stride but won't feel guilty because I never wilfully do damage. Most people aren't wilfully doing it. They are a consequence of the culture. I also don't celebrate when it was someone else who missed. I ask, "Is there a way I can help you?"

"MANUAL TESTING IS DEAD"

Most of the flying parts of an aeroplane are controlled by the autopilot and yet we don't say, "Humans flying an airplane is dead". Why are we doing that with Testing?

The kind of testing the majority of the industry does or has seen is shallow - checking work. Even outside India, I mean. Such a shallow form of checking work was born as an outcome of the distrust people have had on testers for generations now. People equate shallow - checking to manual testing. When they picture a human tester in the mind, they think about someone following a script and doing exactly what the script says. They imagine humans marking pass or fail based on checks.

They don't think of an intelligent human being who influences the project and its people towards a better world. Also because such people in testing are rare and situations might force them out to become a developer, a developer in test or a business analyst.

◎ Chaos

My sympathies to entry level testers. They are threatened even before they have set foot in testing. Someone in fear of losing their job can't perform well and people use it as an opportunity to say, "Hence proved, we should get rid of manual testing".

I put out a post on LinkedIn saying - "If companies paid you less for a switch to automation from manual, would you?" and the majority response was "Yes". Even people who wanted more money in their current jobs said they would trade it for automation any day.

What do you think is the chaos here?

I may have a surprise for you. Such people who are threatened with their jobs learn front end automation or, rather, try to learn front end automation. Driven by fear, their learning isn't good. Their fundamentals aren't good. Their learning is just enough to get to crack automation job interviews. When these people start writing test scripts, they write test code that requires massive maintenance.

They write code around the constraints without fixing the constraints and testability. They feel highly secure going back to the script they wrote and keep changing it to make it green. They love it. That is their way of retaining their job. Management doesn't want to see automation fail. So they will spend more money to fix it every time it breaks. That's even more money than what manual testing was costing them. 3 times more. 5 times in some cases.

⌒ Inner Peace

Most shallow checks should go away from humans. I vote for it. At the same time I am exposed to a certain kind of testing that focuses on finding risks and influencing people that only humans can do. I have experienced the influence it has had on people and the positive impact it can create on customers and users.

Testing = Learning + Discovery + Setup + Experiment Design + Running Tests + Observing + Inferring + Conjecturing + Reporting + Influencing + Unlearning.

We take the Running Tests part and associate it with Humans and think that Manual Testing is dead with Automation. Who would do other aspects such as Discovering, Setup, Experiment Design and Influencing People? Are they automated? They are still human driven. They will remain human driven for a long time to come. So Testing isn't automated. Running tests to some degree is automated.

The industry is in its experimenting phase with Testing. Some experiments are long and take some time to discover the outcomes. I am not reacting to people saying anything against Testing these days. I am letting them say what they want. Deep inside I know that the industry will wake up to reality someday. I just want to be ready for what that day needs from me. I want to be useful in the best possible way. I am building the things required for that day.

- When DSLR was introduced, a new generation of photographers was born.
- When drone cameras were introduced, a new skill was added to photographers.
- No amount of automation will remove the need for photographers.
- If it is fun, humans will do it.
- The best photographers you know will be shooting in manual mode.
- They produce some of the best pictures you and I have enjoyed.
- Manual photography is for experts.
- Manual testing has to get there and it is getting there.
- What a great time to be a manual tester, if you are an expert or want to be one.

Chaos within this peace:

Okay, I get it, some of you don't like to see the word "manual" being used for humans. You want to call it - Exploratory Testing or something else. I think so too. The word "Manual" has a bad background attached to it. We could move away from that word and use a new word which does not have baggage. What is equally important is the value we bring. Manual, Exploratory or Automation. The value we deliver matters. Instead of focusing on value, focusing on the word can become a distraction.

Usage of "manual testing" is like usage of "common sense", in a metaphorical way. The true meaning of common sense is all five senses of a human arriving at one common understanding to help humans move forward. Instead the world uses "common sense" in a totally different context.

"IF YOU DON'T LEARN CODING - YOU CAN'T CONTINUE IN TESTING"

If someone is testing software they need to know how software is built, marketed, sold, used and supported. They need to know the technology layers, backend systems, the domain and the architecture. Since we are living in the era where programmers drive testing, the expectation is such that if you aren't solving a problem through programming, then you aren't one among us.

Programming is one of the most powerful tools ever produced on this earth. Without programming and software I can't imagine how this world would have been.

◎ Chaos

The industry's biggest problem is that there are plenty of testers testing web apps who don't know the technical layers of the application they are testing. Observations made at the front end without co-relating to what has happened in the background aren't useful.

Most testers today are shallow, surface-level sporadic observers. They are being paid every month and they are being given a hike every year driving home a point that what they are doing is giving them growth. After 2 decades of this practice in the industry, people are waking up to the fact that testers need to know technology really deeply.

The industry is doing a pretty bad job of articulating this change. A better (but not necessarily great) alternate than, "Learn coding" could be, "If you aren't deep tech, you won't succeed in testing". The quality of the code many testers write is poor. This is a result of "learn coding" that the industry is doing to itself. Also the chaos is about - what should one do if they don't get coding into their heads. Should they quit testing?

∿ Inner Peace

- I understand testing to be a feedback loop as I have described earlier.
- Feedback is required by many stakeholders in the organization.
- There are two major Heads in a Company.
- Business Head and Technology Head.
- Business requires feedback.
- Technology requires feedback.
- Testers have two choices in their career.
- Be business savvy or be technology savvy.
- Whatever you choose, you need to have a medium depth understanding of the other.
- I have been a business savvy tester in the past.

- I have partnered with people who are tech-savvy and produced some great output together.
- They have benefited from my business savviness and vice versa.
- While I have been business savvy, my testing had enough tech depth required to build credibility with the tech teams. I wrote code too, in bits and pieces.

For example, in 2005, I was a Blackbox Tester for the Real Media Player App on Win CE Mobile. Here is how I approached it:

- Understood the codec support required.
- Understood how these different codecs work.
- Understood the architecture.
- Understood the streaming protocols I am going to be using.
- Understood the different container formats.
- Discovered different audio video standards.
- Read the product code.
- Assessed testability of code.
- Worked with the developers to understand their implementation and the wrappers they wrote.
- Designed tests that would test the architecture, exceptions, claims, streaming latency, scientific analysis of the quality measuring jitters, packet drops, Signal to Noise Ratio etc.
- Paired with developers while they were bug fixing to prevent them and myself from getting into regression around the bug.

- Published my test data with developers to help them do some level of TDD/Unit Testing in ways I understood TDD and Unit Testing back then.

Yet, I consider myself to be business savvy. Being business savvy isn't an excuse to not learn about technology. Someone like Rahul Verma would have gone deeper than me on technical than what I did and yet be business aware. We compliment each other very well.

A tester has to either be super business savvy or super tech-savvy. If someone is in between, the value becomes harder to sell. I have seen super tech people with no business savviness doing damage to the project as much as people who are business savvy but technologically handicapped.

Since there are plenty of tech-savvy testing jobs, a lot of people think programming is their only option to move forward. I think knowing who we are is critical to what we choose. We will suffer quite a lot if we choose something that goes against us

Given that I have chosen what suits me, I am completely at peace with it.

Given that I know who I am not, I partner with people.

I wanted to be a super tester long ago who knows everything. I wanted to be a one man army. Until one day I realized that one man is never an army.

Today, I belong to an army of testers who help each other no matter who gets hired.

"THE ROLE OF A TESTER IS DIMINISHING IN THE AGILE - DEVOPS WORLD"

The intent of Agile & DevOps is aimed to improve the speed, improve the efficiency, make it easy to produce high quality software, ship faster and hence make life easier for people building software. Like the Chinese Whisper Game - by the time intent reaches the majority of the world, the message and purpose gets changed. That is the world we are living in.

I guess people who came up with the Agile Manifesto would keep saying, "This is not what we intended."

◎ Chaos

I do a lot of talks at organizations in India. I ask, "Are you following Agile?" and they say, "Yes" and I follow up with a question, "Really?" and then most of them change the answer "No".

For Agile to work - there needs to be a cultural shift in many companies. The culture is governed by business, product and tech leaders in the org. It has to begin with them. Instead, if they give it out as a mandate to the org to migrate to Agile - it is a disaster waiting to happen.

I noticed an implementation of Agile at a large company where testers were testing what is covered in that particular story and they move onto the next sprint story and focus just on that sprint. No one was testing how these stories interacted with each other. Do you see the risk?

Another implementation. All re-testing to be done by automation and only current sprint testing by humans. While I like the intent to free up humans from regression, forcing a certain practice irrespective of the ground reality, doesn't help. Sometimes we may need to retest a couple of times to learn the behavior of the software.

DevOps practice is an intended faster feedback loop. We read posts like, "Is QA relevant in DevOps world?". Again, threatening the existence of pilots with autopilots. Gets the eyeballs but is impractical for the future. Maybe the kind of QA Testing they have seen needs to die but not the kind of QA Testing it really was meant to be.

∼ Inner Peace

A famous multi-billion dollar organization I worked with made a decision to let go all of its QA Testers. All. Their own employees. Contractors. Testers from vendors. Why? If there are other companies who can work without Testers - why should they?

I was impacted by this decision but I kept my calm. I supported their decision while warning about the potential risks. I loved this decision because I wanted to learn how it pans out. If it really does work great then I have something great to learn from it. I could have used that information to pivot my career into something else.

2 weeks passed. All of them were called back. Why? They hit roadblocks. As a culture they weren't ready for this. A key feedback loop their entire organization was using suddenly disappeared. This made the decision makers on the ground very uncomfortable.

99% of industry is copycat. They think Testers aren't hired in Apple. I was consulting for a large IT Services firm somewhere in Pune and there was a team testing the Apple iTunes Page.

Apple takes a week to publish apps and updates every time they are submitted. I believe they do have enough automated systems but I also believe there are humans sitting somewhere testing if the app submitted meets the necessary App Store Guidelines. It takes a combination of machines and humans to build quality.

As Jerry Weinberg said, "If you compromise quality, you can meet any requirement".

Having experienced and known these stories, I am letting people go through what the multi-billion dollar company went through. I would love every company to try it. Sooner. If it works, good. If it doesn't, they won't be promoting the "We can run without Testers" and causing fear in their own employees.

I have the right patience and time to watch the industry go through it. I just believe we will be hitting a tipping point in 2–3 years where the industry will settle in to a relatively better understanding of Testing. Up until then - I have to keep learning, experimenting, building things of value, building partnerships and enjoy my time here. I'm also preparing for what the tipping point will bring.

MS Dhoni: Calm amidst chaos.

We all need to Rest In Peace even before death.

CHAPTER

COMMUNICATING WITH STAKEHOLDERS WHOSE PRIMARY FOCUS IS NOT TESTING

BUSINESS

Most testers don't know about business. Neither do most developers. Business is not logical most of the time. People wouldn't have started a business if they looked at logic. Programmers and Testers deal with a lot of logic and expect logic from business.

Some business people are about value creation for everyone in the ecosystem. Most business people are those with a mission to solve a customer's problem at large scale. Some business people only focus on money.

- They track topline (revenue) and bottomline (profit).
- Their top problem is the topline (in most large orgs).
- Their next big problem is market share.
- Their problem is competition (for medium to large companies).
- They want to stand on top of the world.
- Most of the times we can't relate to them.
- Starting a business is not being your own boss. It is having everyone around you as your boss.

⊚ Chaos

Were you in a situation where you showed a few blockers and thought the release wouldn't happen, but to your surprise it did? Everyone has been there. Business decisions aren't rationale (to us) all the time.

The fact is testers don't know business. The business doesn't know tech and even the business that knows tech doesn't know testing. The business has sometimes questioned the need for QA and Testing. A lot of non-tech business people who want a product built don't yet understand why they should pay for testing. Since they don't want to pay - they pay less. If you don't invest enough on anything you do, your results won't be satisfactory.

Tech-savvy business people want it fully automated, oblivious to the fact that if too much automation is at the UI layer, the cost of automation maintenance will exceed their budget over time. Automation needs to come at the Dev layer and that is hard to get at scale.

Many large org CIOs have a Key Results Area to show cost savings and increases in profit. Automation in Testing provides the notion of cost saving and letting a few testers go adds up to it. The remaining few QA Testers life becomes hell because they now take the burden of the further reduced test time, team size, resources, and budgets to deliver results that are very hard to deliver hence compromising their lifestyle.

As testers, if we are asked to show business value where we have no clue of business, we will all think of showing it through automation and showing it through the efficiency of test cases executed per hour. Where is the testing here?

A lot of managers in Testing and Development have grown by showing something is now moving faster (even if it was in the wrong direction).

⌁ Inner Peace

What do business people want in their life?

- They want a specific customer pain solved through the product?
- They want customers getting added month on month.
- They want revenue to grow at a certain pace.
- They want profits to grow over a period of time.
- They want to retain paying customers.
- They want their marketing spend to yield more customers.

Any information or bugs I find in software, I assess the impact on:

- Revenue
- User acquisition
- User retention
- User drop off
- Marketing spend usefulness
- Bottom line

I was doing this prior to building my own business. I was so off reality then.

After having started business - my reports became closer to reality.

The acknowledgment from business people is such a high for me as a tester.

Most people in the capacity of business who are not entrepreneurs know two things.

1. Chase a given metric.
2. Cut costs.

Unless their boss loves the testing we do, we are just a cost.

Having understood this I just build things to influence their boss who could understand business or build things that move their metric. Build things = in the testing space. I = the team. It takes time to build influence.

I am also ready to be laid off or fired anytime if I am working with people who think of testing as a cost. I don't bring my emotions when they fire me. It is Business As Usual.

Additional Note:

As a business savvy medium depth tech tester, I have translated my findings into what impacts the business. My bug reporting has business savvy elements while selling bugs to business. I build automation that helps businesses. Note that I didn't say - Test Automation.

As an example, I was brought in as a consultant for 6 weeks to Tesco. Someone was on leave and I was available to fill in. I noticed on day 1 that my output helps the business team make a certain decision at a certain time.

Using that info I built an automation (err, not me, by partnering with a developer who had recently joined and was yet to be assigned to a project) to help the business make decisions faster. This tool we built fetched a lot of appreciation from the business. When the tester whom I replaced came back, I had changed the checking job to a thinking job for the tester. The tester came back and was asked to look at what other tools can be built to help make business decisions faster.

I was re-hired by Tesco for other projects to solve other business problems.

If we haven't touched the business in a positive way, they don't understand our value.

Once we do that they want to expose us to a ton of pain they have and our value significantly grows.

PRODUCT OWNERS AND BUSINESS ANALYST

Product Owners and BA have business accountability. They translate a vision to product requirement. They translate market understanding to product and user requirements. They make inferences from analytics and translate it to what should change in the product. They observe user behavior and define experiences to enhance user value. They also find out what makes people pay for their product.

What do they need from testing?
Isn't testing supposed to report only to tech?

Product Owners and BA's are important stakeholders to Tech Teams. Testing, since it is a feedback loop, is a necessary system for PO and BA's. The business people may not be interacting with Testers as much as PO's and BA's do.

⑥ Chaos

In industries that require a lot of domain understanding, the BAs and POs interact closely with Testers as much as Tech Teams do. For instance, all regulated industries have BAs working closely and reviewing the feedback from Testing. In places where domain understanding isn't a big deal, Test closely works only with Tech.

Even then, the POs need feedback. I noticed that sometimes the POs have set up their own mini feedback loops either by hiring an independent agency or by bringing in one or two testers into the Product Teams.

All seems well - where is the chaos?

Product teams want product feedback from testing but don't have the time to sift through the bug reports and make sense of what needs to change. Testers aren't good at articulating the way PO wants it.

POs and BAs like to be challenged early on in the sprint or cycle rather than later. They need a high level summary of the risks.

Testers who have made a difference to PO and BA teams have had higher growth within companies. But how do we make that impact? There is no material about it. There's a lot of material out there about testing that seldom talks about PO and BA perspectives and values from testing.

∼∼Inner Peace

I have been building testing tools and trying to distribute them. I understand what POs and BAs are going through. Long ago when I built a fresh grad test coach program, I designed it in such a way that people built a product. They thought about a product, wrote code and testing was at the last part of the training program. It took a month to get to testing.

I don't see such coaching happening in the industry so people obviously lack the perspective of a Product Owner and BA. Of course, they gain over a period of time by working closely with them. Not all get it because they think their core deliverable is to run tests and report the pass fail. The automators are more concerned about their own script failure than the product or the owners of it.

Even when I became a Product Owner I was working with my own company testers and thought that they too lacked the perspective. They were reporting good bugs that I could appreciate as a tester but didn't move my needle as a PO.

That's why I started to coach people from the PO perspective of Testing and it happened to be an eye-opener workshop for me and for the Testers I coached.

I am at peace now working with any PO and BAs as I can connect to their pain and report things that matter to them.

Here is one word they care about: "Impact".

You may find a trivial issue but if it impacts the user or customer negatively, they want to know.

The negative here refers to revenue, customer retention and the understanding of the use case itself. You may find a super crash but if the impact on the user base is low or it is a corner case - they will ignore it.

CTO/VP ENGINEERING

These are geeks under pressure. Anything wrong with the org can show up in tech. For instance, these are the people who get the first big pressure to increase velocity. They also have huge shortage of developers to achieve the velocity they need to achieve. That's not to say that more developers mean better speed or quality. It is just the context of the CTO/VP Engineering.

They know what creates better quality code. Not all times that is possible due to pressure that comes to these people from various angles.

If you take a VC funded firm that is competing with another VC funded firm. VCs on both sides would be adding pressure to move faster - overall. You can instantly put more money into digital marketing and bring a ton of loads of people on to your app, but the tech doesn't scale like that. It takes time.

◎ Chaos

Many testers think their job is to find faults of others, err, most likely programmers. This is flawed. However, I have seen people take pride in this flaw.

Many testers go loggerheads with developers. Developers and testers are working towards a common goal. Issues do happen when the culture of engineering or the company is toxic. Note that when two countries go to war it is the soldiers who fight the war, not the people who called the war.

What do the CTO and VP Engineering want from Testers?

They want speed.
They also don't want Testing to become a bottleneck.
They certainly want clean code.
They want good enough engineering practices.

Given that they are under pressure to show velocity or speed, often QA Testing comes up as a bottleneck for them. They can't cut code to show speed. They can cut Testing or speed it up through Automation. They do this up until automation becomes a bottleneck.

Even in the company I am building, unit testing practice isn't as good as I would have liked it to be. I have shared my views and value of unit testing with my CTO and left him to think about it. I also see a lot of companies that have very little, shallow, sporadic efforts on unit testing.

Tech debt hits them hard. Most testers I know don't know tech debt or the impact it has on the project and scalability.

I wrote a post on LinkedIn about unit testing and how the majority of the bugs I found could have been caught in Unit Testing. With close to 1 million views, the post went viral. It kinda shows what the industry's sentiment is about it.

A lot of testers don't know to ask about unit testing. A lot of testers are finding bugs that they shouldn't be.

∿ Inner Peace

I empathize with CTOs and VP Engineering for the pressure they have on faster releases. Speed comes at a certain compromise of quality. When I work on projects I try to assess how much quality can realistically be built in given the speed. I also look at how the whole engineering team (+ PO + Business) owns up the quality.

I don't want to be a superman tester trying to save the company when its practices aren't in the right place. I certainly influence them. I write emails to CTO and VP with my observations. Of course, I have been ignored many times but my job is to escalate and their job is to decide. My job is also to not judge them.

What do the CTOs and VPs need from Testing?

Speed. Get the minimum amount of testing possible to report issues that help them make quick decisions.

This is where an approach like the Rapid Software Testing of James Bach and Michael Bolton can come in very handy. Robert Sabourin also has Just In Time Testing. Many industry experts like them have very focused expert testing approaches and methodologies.

Engineering teams need a lot of automation, but it gets translated in a really bad way where people start getting their heads around, "Let's do Appium because that helps me get my next best job."

They also want Dev + Test as one team.

I will also make a statement. They don't understand Test as much as they do with Dev.

I went through many job posts for VP Engineering. None of it mentioned the word test. However, they would be expected to run Test Engineering as well.

My peace comes with all this understanding. Since I connect with them on their problems I speak very differently as a tester with them. Since I build tools to speed up my testing, I am not becoming a bottleneck for them.

I never partied with people who were like "Can we use this tool so that I can get my next best job?"

Largely at peace.

We fear becoming ourselves.

CHAPTER

LIFE AND CAREER IN THE TEST PYRAMID

TEST PYRAMIDS: WHAT ARE THEY?

99% of the people who talk about the test pyramid end up drawing a triangle while explaining it.

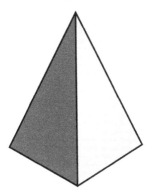

There are darker sides in the pyramid. 95% of the people live on the darker side.

This is a great reference point that lists test pyramids
http://www.testingreferences.com/here_be_pyramids.php

Pradeep Soundararajan
Founder CEO of Moolya Testing & App Achhi
2w

I completed 16 years in testing.

95% of the bugs I found were supposed to have been found during unit testing.

It amazes me that I built a career out of finding things I was not supposed to.

Long live unit testing.

8,217 · 292 Comments

There must be a reason why so many people were interacting with this post.

As far as I know, unit and integration testing is fundamental to getting code quality right. Yet, the practice is to push quality to the last moment in the hands of testers.

I did a talk recently at a developer conference in a room full of 100+ developers. I asked for a show of hands.

"How many of you do unit testing?"
Less than 50% of the hands went up.

"How many of those who raised your hands don't like doing unit testing but are doing it as an obligation?"

50% of the previous 50% hands went up.

A lot of people think this is an India specific problem and not a global problem.

Not true. I have seen this in most global companies who have set up their shops in India. It can't be true that they do a different approach in America and a different approach in India. If they do that, they are merging bad quality code to their locally brewed good quality code which results in poor quality code.

My guess is that the practice is global. Good or bad.

ORG CULTURES IMPACT QUALITY

The largest contributor to quality is the org culture. Culture is set by the C, V and D level people in any organization but work is done by everyone else. Directions are set by them while speed is delivered by everyone else.

I have heard a lot of talk about shifting testing left. What we should ideally be doing is shifting quality everywhere. Agile implementations that begin with a CXO looking at it like a task to be completed by X amount of time, is a clear recipe for disaster. There are also cases where it went wrong because of the people on the ground. It only shows everyone is equally responsible. Shift testing everywhere. Shift quality everywhere!

Towards the end of 2019, I was consulting for a large company headquartered in Europe with a huge IT presence in India, claimed to have fully transitioned to DevOps and had no testers.

I asked the delivery managers, as a student, and out of sheer curiosity to learn

"Why am I here?"

And their response, "Well, we seem to have regression issues."

"Why do you think that is happening?"

… "Our developers who test as a part of DevOps don't want to test and hence some tests are getting missed."

"How are you then mitigating this risk?"

…"We have a small team of testers who are covering up for it."

"I thought you started by saying you don't have testers."

…"Yeah, we don't have them on our rolls."

I told them that the only way I can help them is by helping them fix their culture and that I may have to speak to their reporting and their skip level boss.

Their CXO might be living in a belief that everyone in their org is testing and hence they have successfully solved the problem of hiring dedicated testers. There's a lot of real change that has to begin from the top. The bottom is just a symptom of the problem that is at the top.

In the company I founded, only when I pointed to myself, the culture went through a change. I could have easily told people to do something different and they would have done it. Nothing would have changed. Their life would have become bad and hence my life would have become miserable because my ship would have hit an iceberg.

There are many companies that are heading right towards the iceberg. I hate to say that some good people in their org are trying to do all the hard work to avoid it but yet it will happen.

I know companies in India that decided to get rid of all testers. There are companies who shut shop and let all their people go. This one isn't that story. This is a story where they thought they could do without testers and later realized they could not. They had to rely more on testers.

This should have been news. I really think it should have.

Why did this happen? Their culture wasn't ready to take it.

Unless we fix our org culture, no amount of test process improvement, no amount of automation or A.I. is going to make any significant impact on the quality of software we produce.

To change org culture we need skills to influence people. Influencing people isn't a skill listed on 99.99 percent of the resume' of most people in tech. Those who code or test, whoever it may be, are in the business of influencing people around the, through their code. through their tests.

DECISIONS IN CAREER

Most people struggle to make decisions if they have multiple offers in front of them. They don't know what is good for them. Since they don't know what is good for them, they seem to go by brand, money, to a certain extent and culture + people they are working with become secondary.

What would more money and no peace do to someone in the long term?

It would not lead to satisfaction. It leads to a midlife crisis. It leads to feeling void most of the time. Especially towards month end where one neither has money nor has satisfaction. One might end up yearning for something that they know they don't have in their current job.

If I ever were to look for a job again in my life, I would be looking at an org who understands, appreciates and is making sincere efforts to get the culture of product and engineering right.

I would think that my employer is the test pyramid and org culture.

I would give myself a title of "Problem Solver".

I would like to understand the skills of the people in the org and would like to build skills that are complementary to them.

I would think that if I have built influence to help people in the company build high quality software without having to hurt each other, I would have a great satisfying moment in my career. At that moment even if my official title is Junior Tester or a Junior Developer, I would feel I am on the top when everyone else feels they are on the top. Being there alone isn't a success.

Oh, and one more thing. Rahul Verma and I compliment each other really well. Avinash Nishant and I compliment each other extremely well. Together we look very strong as a team.

I would look for a partnership to solve problems. Without a partnership we are all broken pieces who feel lonely and find addiction to something useless as the best alternate.

I built a tool that helps in some level of career analysis. There are 500+ testers who have taken it and 27 of them sent emails to me that it is very helpful to them. You should try it out: http://tinyurl. com/careeranalysis

Life = signal + noise.
What we focus on gets amplified.

CO-AUTHOR THIS BOOK WITH ME?

CO-AUTHOR THIS BOOK WITH ME?

Write your own chapter of what brings you inner peace amidst the chaos. Send me your chapter to pradeep.srajan@gmail.com so that I can learn from it.

- What is the chaos that surrounds you in testing?
- What is your contribution to the chaos?
- What situations and conversations have put you out of your calmness?
- How do you plan to bring peace to yourselves in each of those contexts?
- What answers are you searching for?
- How do you recognize the answer that gives you peace?
- Who are you working with and what should you understand about them?
- What are you trying to change? Why?
- What do you fear? Why do you fear it?
- What should you be doing to get out of those fears?
- How do you plan to build partnerships at work?
- What business problems should you be solving for your org?
- What is the value of what you do? How do you know that?
- How can you make it easy for people to work with you and give you feedback?

We become the opportunities we did not take.

A THANK YOU LIST

To you, for being the co-author of this book.

My 8 year old daughter, Adhvika, who was playing around when I was focused on writing this book at home, dropped by and asked me what I was doing and I replied, "I am writing a book" and then she said, "No, you are not. You are typing a book." Thanks to her for helping me see that I did not "write" a book.

My wife, my mom, my in-laws, my brother and his family for helping me become more human and humane as days pass by.

My dad who passed away a few years ago and yet lives through our family.

My business partner Avinash Nishant for taking my phone calls at odd times. Also the one who taught me how fulfilling business partnerships can be.

My mentors, Sriram Tadimal and Subinder Khurana for the guidance.

To Kavitha Parmesh and Smitha Prabhakar who extended great support at work.

The people at Notion Press who helped me bring this book out.

The editor at Notion Press, whose preference is to be just called the "editor."

Thanks to James Bach and Michael Bolton for buying me a laptop and a table in 2007 when I didn't have one. Also for coaching me over the years and then letting me be myself. Rapid Software Testing materials and exercises to help me explore myself in testing. Michael Bolton's blog is worth more than several books in testing.

Jerry Weinberg for helping me feel good about myself by letting me collaborate with him and review his book Perfect Software and Other Illusions About Testing which I highly recommend.

Elizabeth Hendrickson for knowing a lot and being calm. She facilitated simple and powerful learning exercises for me in testing and communication. Her book Explore It is a powerful book on exploratory testing that I strongly recommend.

Ben Simo to have been a friend and the genius I know in Testing.

Robert Sabourin for being my grandpa and asking very practical questions about testing plus his coaching and consulting work that is a masterpiece.

Karen Johnson took the earliest bet on me to engage me on a project she was consulting on.

Rosie Sherry to have collaborated with me on a few projects during her early Software Testing Club (pre-Ministry of Testing) days and for building the MoT in awesome ways with Richard Bradshaw.

Jon Bach for finding something different in me that everyone else missed. For coming into my life, telling a story about me and disappearing. Jonathan Livingston Seagull of my life.

Vipul Kocher to have given me a few projects when I badly needed one in life.

Rahul Verma for the partnership we have enjoyed and for the person he is.

Ramit Manohar for supporting me whenever I have asked for it.

Sigge Birgisson for being a great friend and for inspiring me with his stature and thoughts.

Maria Kademo for the faith she put in me for conference talks.

Sridhar Krishnamurthy and Ravi Joshi for coaching and mentoring me in my early career days.

Parimala Hariprasad, Sharath Byregowda, Sunil Kumar T for the friendship and supporting me throughout.

Dhanasekar Subramanian for the many number of conversations, beer and whisky.

Pallavi Sharma, Chidambaram Ganesan and Shivaprasad for beta reading this book and giving me confidence, critique and suggestions that helped me.

Perez Ababa, Huib Schoots and Paul Holland for believing in me and Moolya.

Adam Goucher for consistent motivation and reminders of value.

Johanna Rothman for her inspiration and books on hiring technical people.

Alan Richardson for his great work, training materials and tools.

Fiona Charles for having shared her consulting stories with me.

Paul Carvalho for having good thoughts on testing and life.

Anand Bagmar for supporting me and complimenting me when I needed it.

Angie Jones for her inspiration and great work on Test Automation University.

Testers in India who give me their energy and love, making me look useful.

Testers outside of India who put in a lot of faith and support.

To my friends at school and college who invested in me.

To my servant leadership team Chandini Mokhthar, Vaisakh VL, Abilash Hari, Prantik Coomar, Surendra Katperi and Mohan Ram for their phenomenal support.

To the people in Moolya and AppAchhi who I serve and are the people who make me look good.

Do you know when to stop?